A WINNING SKILLS BOOK

You Can Handle Criticism and Rejection!

Joy Berry

Illustrated by Bartholomew

Joy Berry Enterprises

Copyright © Joy Berry, 2022
Originally Published 2013

All rights are reserved.

No part of this book can be duplicated or used without the prior written permission of the copyright owner, except for the use of brief quotations from the book.

For inquiries or permission requests contact the publisher.

Published by Joy Berry Enterprises
www.joyberryenterprises.com

Joy Berry
Enterprises

You can handle criticism and rejection by learning about
- constructive criticism,
- destructive criticism,
- considering the source,
- dealing with people who are not qualified to criticize you,
- receiving constructive criticism,
- responding to constructive criticism,
- four steps for handling destructive criticism,
- feeling rejected,
- minimizing the effects of rejection, and
- overcoming rejection.

INTRODUCTION

Criticism is a judgmental evaluation of someone or something.

Criticism can be constructive or destructive.

Constructive criticism can have a positive effect on the person who is being criticized. The purpose of constructive criticism is to help rather than to hurt others.

Constructive criticism usually reveals something that needs to be changed. When the person who has been criticized makes the necessary change, he or she can grow and become a better person.

For criticism to be constructive, it should be directed at things that can be changed and said in a kind and considerate way.

DESTRUCTIVE CRITICISM

Destructive criticism usually has a negative effect on the person who is being criticized. The purpose of destructive criticism is often to hurt rather than help others.

When nothing can be done to improve something, it is pointless to criticize it. Criticism directed at things that cannot be changed is usually destructive.

When someone criticizes you, it is important to "consider the source." This means evaluating the person to determine whether or not he or she is qualified to criticize you.

People who criticize you should be **intelligent and wise** enough to make judgments about you.

People who criticize you must be **trustworthy.** They must care about you and have your best interests at heart.

People who criticize you must have **pure motives.** Their purpose in criticizing you should be to help you, not to hurt you.

People who criticize you must **be accurate.** They must have facts or other information to support what they say about you.

People should not be expressing their own **emotional problems** when they criticize you. People who are depressed, anxious or upset, might express their uncomfortable feelings by criticizing you. This kind of criticism has nothing to do with you and cannot help you in any way.

People should not be expressing their own **physical problems** when they criticize you. People who are hungry, tired, or sick might express their discomfort by criticizing you. This kind of criticism has nothing to do with you and cannot help you in any way.

People should not be **projecting their own faults** onto you when they criticize you. Sometimes people are unaware of having a certain fault that is unacceptable to them. At the same time, they accuse others of having the fault. This kind of criticism has nothing to do with you and cannot help you in any way.

To be qualified to criticize you, people must
- be intelligent and wise,
- be trustworthy,
- have pure motives, and
- be accurate.

To be qualified to criticize you, people must not use criticism to
- express their own emotional problems,
- express their own physical problems, or
- project their faults onto you.

18 ◼ DEALING WITH PEOPLE WHO ARE NOT QUALIFIED TO CRITICIZE YOU

Sometimes when you consider the source, you will determine that the person criticizing you is **not** qualified to do so. When this happens, ask the person to stop criticizing you.

DEALING WITH PEOPLE WHO ARE NOT QUALIFIED TO CRITICIZE YOU

Sometimes someone who is not qualified to criticize you will continue to do so even after you have asked him or her to stop. When this happens, try to ignore what is being said or separate yourself from the person.

RECEIVING CONSTRUCTIVE CRITICISM

Most people are open to receiving constructive criticism when
- they are feeling well emotionally and physically,
- they are not preoccupied, and
- they receive it in private.

Sometimes someone might want to share some constructive criticism with you when you are not feeling well physically or emotionally. Your mind most likely will be on your problems and not on what is being said. If this happens, explain how you feel and ask the person to share the criticism with you when you are feeling better.

Sometimes someone might want to share some constructive criticism with you when you are busy doing something else. Your attention most likely will be focused on what you are doing and not on what is being said. If this happens, explain that you are preoccupied and ask the person to wait and share the criticism with you when you can give your full attention.

Sometimes someone might want to share some constructive criticism with you in front of other people. This could become embarrassing for everyone. If this happens, ask the person to wait until the criticism can be shared privately.

RESPONDING TO CONSTRUCTIVE CRITICISM

To benefit from constructive criticism, you need to respond to it appropriately. To do this, follow these six steps:

Step 1: Listen carefully while you are being criticized.

Try to avoid interrupting when someone is criticizing you. Instead of defending yourself or making excuses for whatever is being criticized focus on what is being said.

Step 2: Thank the person who has criticized you.

Since constructive criticism can be beneficial it is important to make people feel comfortable about sharing it with you. If you make people feel uncomfortable about offering constructive criticism, they might stop doing it. This could cause you to miss out on some wonderful opportunities to grow and become a better person.

Step 3: Carefully consider the criticism you have received.

Try to determine whether or not the criticism is **valid.** Consider whether or not it is true and is about something that can be corrected. Keep an open mind and examine the information that has been presented. It might help to talk to several other qualified people and get their opinions about the criticism.

Step 4: Decide what you need to do about the criticism.

If you determine that the criticism is not valid, you will **not** need to make any change. However, if you determine that the criticism is valid, you will need to decide exactly what change needs to be made.

Step 5: Follow through with whatever you have decided to do.

Make whatever change is necessary.

Step 6: Talk to the person who criticized you.

If you decided to make a change, the person who criticized you most likely will appreciate knowing about it.

If you decided against making a change, it would be good to let the person know. Then he or she will not feel ignored and won't continue criticizing you.

Just as constructive criticism can be helpful, destructive criticism can be harmful.

Destructive criticism can damage your self-esteem and confidence.

This can cause you to become less productive and keep you from achieving you full potential. To avoid the negative effects of destructive criticism, you need to handle it appropriately. To do this, follow these four steps:

Step 1: Let the person who is criticizing you know that his or her destructive criticism is unacceptable.

Look the person in the eye, and explain that you feel his or her criticism is not valid. Then, tell the person why you think this is true.

Step 2: Tell the person who is criticizing you how the criticism makes you feel.

Let the person know if the criticism has hurt or upset you.

Step 3: Stop listening to the criticism.

Finally, ask the person who is criticizing you to stop. If he or she will not stop, ignore the criticism or separate yourself from the person.

Step 4: Put the criticism aside.

Avoid thinking about the criticism. Replace it with positive thoughts about yourself.

It will help if you spend time with people who genuinely like you and who will help you identify and affirm your positive qualities.

FEELING REJECTED

Sometimes being criticized can cause you to feel rejected. Feeling rejected means feeling unloved or unwanted.

Feeling rejected can have a negative effect on you. It can cause you to feel inferior. It can lower you self-confidence and affect your ability to achieve. This can make you feel unhappy.

MINIMIZING THE EFFECTS OF REJECTION

You can minimize the negative effects of feeling rejected by realizing these things:

Every human being is valuable and deserves to be accepted by others.

Even thought human beings are valuable, they are not perfect.

Everyone has ways in which he or she can improve. Everyone misbehaves and has problems at one time or another.

Healthy, intelligent people believe in the value of every human being. At the same time, they realize that human beings are not perfect.

Sometimes healthy, intelligent people reject misbehavior or problems in other people. However, they do not reject the people themselves.

People who reject others rather than their misbehavior are not acting intelligently or reasonably.

Therefore, you must not think that something is wrong with you if someone rejects you. Instead you need to realize that something is wrong with the attitude of the person who is rejecting you.

Sometimes you can persuade people to stop rejecting you.

If a person's rejection of you is based on inaccurate information, it might help to talk with the person. This can give you a chance to correct any misconceptions and might alter how the person feels toward you.

If a person's rejection is based on valid criticism of you, it might help to make some necessary changes. Doing this might alter how the person feels toward you.

Sometimes, no matter what you say or do, you cannot make a person stop rejecting you.

When this happens you need to do several things.
- Remember that you are a human being and, even though you are not perfect, you are still valuable.

- Remember, it is the person who rejects you—not you—who has the problems.

- Avoid being around any person who rejects you.

- Spend time with people who like and appreciate you.

CONCLUSION

You can benefit from learning how to recognize whether criticism is constructive or destructive.

You can also benefit from learning to recognize whether a person is qualified to criticize you.

CONCLUSION

Remember, if someone who is qualified criticizes you and you receive the criticism appropriately, you can grow and become a better person.

www.ingramcontent.com/pod-product-compliance
Lightning Source LLC
Chambersburg PA
CBHW081408070526
44583CB00020B/2732